CONTENTS

INTRODUCTION

A short history

Snowboarding is the ultimate sporting success story. In just 30 years it has grown from nothing into an official Olympic event practised by millions. The secret of its success is simple – snowboarding is great fun.

The origins of snowboarding

The origins of snowboarding lie in skateboarding and surfing. The sport was developed by enthusiasts who wanted to transport the thrill of riding waves or skate parks to the mountains.

The earliest snowboard was called the **Snurfer**, invented in the mid-1960s by an American surfer called Sherman Poppen. It had a primitive design and looked a bit like a water-ski without **bindings**. The rider held a rope attached to the front of the board for balance and enjoyed a frightening ride down the slope.

There is no limit to the fun you can have snowboarding. Practise hard enough and before long you too will be enjoying the thrill of flying through the air.

Radical Sports
SNOWBOARDING

Andy fraser••••••••••••

Heinemann
LIBRARY

www.heinemann.co.uk
Visit our website to find out more information about **Heinemann Library** books.

To order:
 Phone 44 (0) 1865 888066
 Send a fax to 44 (0) 1865 314091
Visit the Heinemann Bookshop at www.heinemann.co.uk to browse our catalogue and order online.

First published in Great Britain by Heinemann Library, Halley Court, Jordan Hill, Oxford OX2 8EJ, a division of Reed Educational and Professional Publishing Ltd.

Heinemann is a registered trademark of Reed Educational & Professional Publishing Limited.

OXFORD   MELBOURNE   AUCKLAND
JOHANNESBURG   BLANTYRE   GABORONE
IBADAN   PORTSMOUTH NH (USA)   CHICAGO

© Reed Educational and Professional Publishing Ltd 2000

500 537133

Designed by Celia Floyd
Illustrations by Jeff Edwards
Originated by HBM Print Ltd, Singapore
Printed in Hong Kong by Wing King Tong

ISBN 0 431 03678 0 (hardback)
04 03 02 01 00
10 9 8 7 6 5 4 3 2 1

ISBN 0 431 03687 X (paperback)
04 03 02 01 00
10 9 8 7 6 5 4 3 2 1

British Library Cataloguing in Publication Data

Fraser, Andy
  Snowboarding. – (Radical sports)
  1. Snowboarding – Juvenile literature
  I. Title
  796.9

Acknowledgements

The Publishers would like to thank the following for permission to reproduce photographs:

Allsport, p. 26 (Shaun Botterill), p. 27 (Brian Bahr); Burton Snowboards, pp. 5, 6, 8, 9 top, 11 (helmet, hat and socks), 21 (Scott Needham), 23; CHOD, courtesy of Whitelines Magazine, p. 7; K2, p. 4; Nick Hamilton, courtesy of Whitelines Magazine, pp. 24, 28, 29; Snowboard Klinik, p. 22; Steven King, pp. 9 bottom, 10-19; Stockfile: Stephen Behr pp. 20, 25.

Cover photograph reproduced with permission of Whitelines

Our thanks to Roger Hughes of the British Snowboard Association for his comments in the preparation of this book. Thanks also to Anna Lawlor, Hamish Duncan, James and Thomas Reynolds and Sam Walker who kindly appeared in the technique photographs. Thanks to Gary Baker, Mark Chesterfield and all the staff at the Tamworth Snowdome and to Diane Dutton of the British Snowboard Association.

Every effort has been made to contact copyright holders of any material reproduced in this book. Any omissions will be rectified in subsequent printings if notice is given to the Publisher.

Any words appearing in the text in bold, **like this**, are explained in the Glossary.

This book aims to cover all the essential techniques of this radical sport but it is important when learning a new sport to get expert tuition and to follow any manufacturers' instructions.

Snowboard pioneer Jake Burton wearing one of his boards. The sport he helped invent is now one of the fastest growing in the world.

Special developments
In the 1970s the idea was taken a step further by such pioneers as American, Jake Burton, and the USA skateboard champion, Tom Sims. Bindings to attach the feet to the board were added and the boards were made lighter and more responsive.

In the early days snowboarders were not welcomed by skiers. They were even prevented from riding **ski lifts** or banned from resorts altogether. But over the years the sport has become accepted and skiers and boarders now share the **pistes**.

Today's sport
Snowboarding continues to grow and evolve. Each season new events and technical developments come along to raise it to an even more advanced level. The number of riders jumping aboard continues to increase, and nearly half of all boarders are aged between six and seventeen. So don't get left behind, get boarding.

THE BOARD

The right board for you

To enjoy snowboarding you need the right kind of board. They may look similar but they don't all perform in the same way. Don't just choose the one with the most colourful design.

The alpine board ····················➤

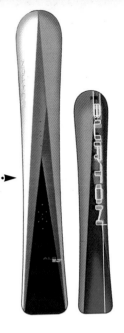

The **alpine** board is designed for speed. It is narrow with a curved **nose** and flat **tail**. It is stiff for stability at high speeds and its long edges help it carve through the snow. Experts use alpine boards for **slalom** races so they can make fast, precise turns as they zigzag between gates.

The freestyle board

This board is for jumping and tricks. It is shorter and fatter than the alpine version. It is called a **twin-tip** because it is the same at both ends, which means you can spin it round and travel backwards. **Freestyle** boards are used for competitions like the **halfpipe**.

The freeride board

The **freeride** is for all types of terrain. It is long enough for neat turns but still flexible enough for tricks. If you fancy a bit of everything and don't want to specialize, this is the one for you.

BOARD TIPS

Choose a board to suit you. If you have big feet and a narrow board your heels will drag in the snow as you turn. If you have small feet and the board is too wide, turning will be difficult. The heavier or taller you are, the longer the board you will need. Always ask for advice.

Board design

The snowboard is a sandwich of different layers. The inner core is made of wood, foam or aluminium. This is strengthened with a covering of fibreglass strands. The logo and design are laid on top and sealed with a transparent top coat. The underside is covered with a clear material called **P-tex**, which helps the board glide smoothly. The board's edges are made of hardened steel and must be sharp for turning.

Logo and design covered with a transparent topcoat ————

Fibreglass covering ————

Inner core ————

Steel board edge ————

Fibreglass covering ————

P-tex coat ————

LEASHES

 Leashes are not just for dogs. Snowboards have no brakes and if you leave them on a slope they will speed off, endangering other skiers and boarders. When you put the board on, attach the leash to your boot or leg before you do anything else.

Turning and jumping puts boards under intense pressure so they have to be tough. This rider pushes his freestyle board to the limit in the halfpipe.

BOOTS AND BINDINGS

As with boards, your choice of boots and **bindings** is determined by the style of snowboarding you want to do. Only **alpine** boards use **hard boots**, so if you prefer the idea of **freestyle** or **freeriding** then **soft boots** are for you.

Soft boots and freestyle bindings

As you would expect, soft boots are more comfortable than hard boots. They are made of rubber and leather but are still strong enough to support the feet. Boots are connected to the board by freestyle bindings made of polycarbon or alloys, which hold the foot in place with straps tightened by clips.

Hard boots and plate-bindings

This system is only used with alpine boards for **carving** at speed. Metal bindings hold the boot on by the heel and toe and are fastened with a clip at the front. The boot itself is made of hard plastic and has several straps that can be tightened up.

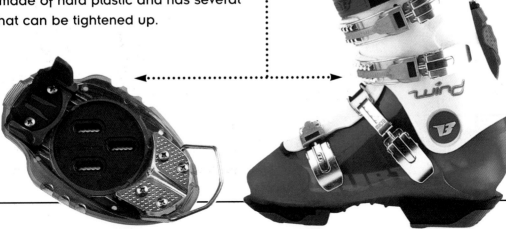

Step-in binding

This is the latest development in boot technology and takes the effort out of putting on your board. A special boot and binding combination allows the boarder to lock into the bindings just by stepping onto the board. To step out all the rider has to do is release a catch.

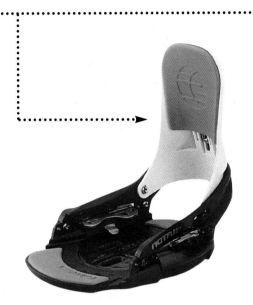

Choosing boots

Wear thick socks when trying on boots and make sure your toes have room to wiggle. Have both feet measured and keep the boots on for at least five minutes. Walk around in them to see how comfortable they are. People usually need boots that are a size bigger than normal shoes. If they hurt after five minutes then imagine how sore your feet will be after a whole day on the slopes. Don't fasten your boots or bindings too tightly – you don't want your fun on the slopes to be hampered by blistered feet.

This boy is choosing boots. Helped by an expert, he spends plenty of time trying them for size and making sure the fit is just right.

THE RIGHT CLOTHES

For successful boarding you need the right clothing. It doesn't matter how good you are – if you are cold or uncomfortable you will not have any fun. Snowboard clothing has been influenced by the loose-fitting clothes that skateboarders wear, so you can usually tell boarders apart from skiers just by what they are wearing.

Eyewear

It's always bright in the mountains, even on an overcast day. Goggles or sunglasses improve visibility and protect the eyes from the glare of the snow. Eyewear should have proper UV-filters to stop harmful ultraviolet rays damaging the eyes.

Bumbag or rucksack

You will need something to carry your essential equipment in, such as sunscreen, food and goggles.

Jacket

Jackets should be warm and waterproof, with a hood and zipped pockets. They should be made of a breathable material that allows sweat and heat to escape but keeps snow and rain out.

Gloves

Snowboarders' hands come into contact with the snow a lot. Whether you are pushing yourself up after a fall or trailing your hand on the ground as you **carve** stylish turns, you need a good pair of well-padded, waterproof gloves.

Snow pants

These should be waterproof and loose-fitting to give you room to move. It helps if they are padded around the knees and backside.

Thick socks

There is nothing worse than cold feet to ruin a boarder's day, so make sure you have thick thermal socks.

Helmet

Even the best snowboarders cannot help falling over every now and then, so it is important to protect yourself by wearing a helmet. Most body heat is lost through the head, so on a cold mountain a hat is a must.

 TOP TIP

It may be cold up on the mountain but the risk of sunburn is high. The sun's rays reflect up off the snow so always use a high protection factor cream on the face and a total sun block on the lips.

Wrist guards

To cut down the risk of a break or sprain wear **wrist guards**.

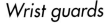

Knee and elbow pads

Protect your knees and elbows with special pads that can be worn under your clothing.

Clothing tips

Weather in the mountains is unpredictable and bright sunshine can quickly be replaced by blizzards. It's better to be too warm than too cold, so wear several layers on top. Thermal underwear gives an extra layer of warmth in cold conditions.

KEEPING FIT AND HEALTHY

It's important to prepare your body for any hard physical activity, so make sure you spend at least 15 minutes stretching thoroughly. Snowboarding uses the same muscles as most other sports so the warm-up is similar.

Warming up

Run on the spot for 10 minutes to get your blood pumping and your muscles warm.

Hips

Hold your arms out in front of you and rotate at the waist to one side and then the other. Next, with your hands on your hips, lean over to one side and then the other. Finally, rotate your hips slowly to stretch your groin muscles.

Hamstring stretch

With your legs apart, reach down and touch the ground between your toes. Then touch your left foot with both hands, come up and do the same with the right foot.

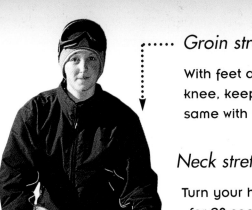

Groin stretch

With feet apart turn to the right side and bend your right knee, keeping the left leg straight. Hold and then do the same with the other leg.

Neck stretches ·······························►

Turn your head to one side and hold it for 20 seconds, then turn it the other way and do the same. Next, bend your neck so your chin is on your chest. Hold it but do not bounce. Never bend your neck backwards, as this can damage it.

Warming down

Warming down is important as your muscles can get tight, increasing the risk of damage the next time you take to the slopes. Jog on the spot or take a brisk walk.

NUTRITION

 When you are doing any physical activity, your body needs lots of energy to function properly. The main source of energy comes from carbohydrates such as cereals, rice, bread, potatoes and pasta.

 Give yourself some energy before boarding with a light meal that might consist of toast, porridge, or a small dish of pasta. Keep your fluid level up by drinking water regularly. Carry snack food with you on the **piste** – a banana, sultanas or muesli bar are ideal.

YOUR FIRST LESSON

What to expect

You can't learn to snowboard without taking a few knocks. In fact, for the first few hours you will be doing little else. But once you start to master the technique, you will conquer the slopes in no time at all. Save yourself time – and bruising – by taking a few one-to-one lessons with a qualified snowboard instructor.

Getting into the binding

When strapping in always attach your **leash** first, so that the board can't run away. Then start by securing the front foot into the **binding**. It helps to sit on the ground and anchor the board by digging the **uphill edge** into the snow.

For comfort and performance your boots must be flat and in the centre of the bindings. Before you step in, brush away any snow from the bottom of your boots or the bindings. Fasten the ankle strap first as this will pull the boot into the binding, and then fasten the toe strap.

This is the best way to strap in. Sitting down, the rider digs the board into the snow to hold it steady and then fastens the bindings.

Basic riding stance

The basic snowboard **stance** is very similar to skateboarding or surfing. The rider stands sideways-on with one foot towards the front of the board and one towards the back. The rider is flexed at the knees and ankles, but not the hips, and the weight is placed equally on both feet. The leading hand points forwards over the **nose** and the trailing hand points backwards over the **tail**.

Are you regular or goofy?

Regular means your left foot is forward and **goofy** means your right foot is forward. As a general rule you should make your strongest foot your back foot. For example, if you kick a ball with your right foot, then this should be your back foot.

This is the basic stance. The rider has the weight evenly shared over both feet for balance.

Balancing exercises

To get used to the strange sensation of being on a board, it helps to practise balancing. Start off by skating forwards on a flat slope with just your front foot in the binding. Then walk up the hill, using your free foot and the **toeside** edge of the board for grip. Once you have strapped in and are standing up, practise rocking onto the nose and onto the tail and **edging** the board on the toe and heel sides.

These riders both have different stances. The rider on the right is goofy (right foot forward) and the rider on the left is regular (left foot forward).

THE BASIC SKILLS

How to fall

Falling while snowboarding is completely different to falling off skis. The **bindings** keep you attached to the board so that if the board gets stuck in the snow you can be thrown in some strange directions.

It's important to know how to fall, because you will be falling down a lot and you need to minimize the risk of injury. Try to take the sting out of the fall by guarding your face with your forearms. Make your hands into fists to protect your wrists. If you can, keep a low centre of gravity by bending your knees so you have less distance to fall and lift the snowboard clear of the snow.

As you go over, the instinctive reaction is to put out your hands to break the fall, which is why injuries to the wrist and fingers are common in snowboarding. To cut down the risk of a break or sprain wear **wrist guards**. Protect your knees and elbows with special pads which can be worn under your clothing. A crash helmet is a must.

This is the safest way to fall. The rider's fists are clenched to protect the fingers and wrists and the forearms take the force of the fall.

Getting up

From a sitting position, bring the board as close to your body as possible, grab the front of the board with one hand and use the other hand to push yourself up. For beginners it's easier to get up when you are facing up the hill. Grab the front knee, bring it into your chest and roll round, then push yourself up with your fists.

Stopping

To stop or slow down, turn the board sideways-on to the hill and then scrape down the slope on your **uphill edge**. If you're doing a **heelside** turn then dig the heelside edge in by lifting your toes. If you're doing a **toeside** turn then dig in the edge by lifting your heels.

This rider shows the easiest way to get up. Facing the slope, he pushes himself up with his fists until he is standing up and ready to ride.

Stopping on the heelside edge. Using his outstretched arms for balance, the rider scrapes downhill with the board side-on to the slope until he comes to a standstill.

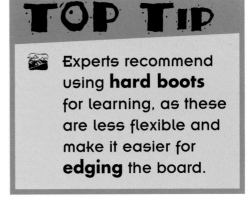

TOP TIP

Experts recommend using **hard boots** for learning, as these are less flexible and make it easier for **edging** the board.

IMPORTANT TURNS

Before you can become a good boarder, you have
to master the basics.

A straight run

Once you are familiar with the feel of the board, make
a straight run down a gentle slope and allow the board
to come to a stop naturally.

The side-slip

This must be learned as it's the boarder's way of
braking. The rider can **side-slip** when facing up or
down the slope by keeping the board at right
angles to the **fall line**. On the **toeside** edge
(facing uphill), lower the heels to pick up speed
and raise them to slow down. On the **heelside**
edge (facing downhill), lower the toes for speed
and raise them to slow down.

The falling leaf

This teaches you how to use your weight to turn the
board. As you side-slip, move your weight onto the right
foot to sweep downhill to the right, then onto the left foot to
change direction and sweep across to the left. The winding left
to right movement is like a leaf falling to the ground. This can
be done with the rider facing either up the slope or down
the slope.

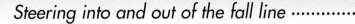

Steering into and out of the fall line

With your board pointing across the slope, gradually move your weight onto the front foot. Your board will start to turn downhill. To stop, increase pressure on the uphill edge and turn the board across the slope.

Traversing

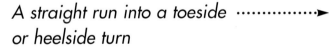

From a side-slip, use a weight transfer to guide the board across the slope on your **toe-edge**. Then go back the other way on your **heeledge**.

A straight run into a toeside or heelside turn

With your weight centred, run straight down the hill. Then transfer your weight to the front foot and raise your heeledge by flexing or pushing your knees forward and rotating the board to make a toeside turn. To make a heelside turn transfer the weight to the front foot and lift the toe-edge by raising your toes while keeping your knees flexed and sit back slightly.

These turns can be linked. Between each turn bring your weight back to the centre and rise up by straightening your legs.

CATCHING A LIFT

Catching your first lift is not easy, but if you are going to come down you have to learn how to go up first.

Drag lifts

Drag lifts pull you up the slope on your board. These take the form of **button lifts** or **T-bars**, depending on the country you are in.

1   Take your back foot out of the **binding** and **scoot** slowly up to the pick-up point.

2   Take the button or T-bar with your leading hand and put it between your legs.

3   Rest your back leg on the space between the front and rear binding. It helps to have a rubber **stomp mat** on the board to stop your boot from slipping off sideways.

4   Keep your board flat and relax as you are pulled uphill. Lean back a little to stop the lift from pulling you off balance.

5   Wait until you reach the very end of the lift then pull the button or T-bar out from between your legs and gently release it. Glide to a halt before putting your boot back into the binding.

Getting on a drag lift at a dry ski slope.

Chair lifts

1   Take your back foot out of the binding and scoot slowly up to the take-off point. Turn and face the chair. As it approaches put your hand out to stop it knocking you over and then sit down.

2   As soon as you are under way pull down the safety bar and rest your board on the footrest.

3   Lift the safety bar as you approach the top of the lift. Push off gently with your hand and, with your back foot on the stomp mat, glide to a halt before strapping back in.

Keep one foot free of the binding when getting off and on a chair lift.

SAFETY FIRST

🏔 It is dangerous to fool around on lifts. If you try to jump or **slalom** as you are being pulled you will fall off. This is embarrassing and you could slide back down the slope towards those coming up behind you. Always take out your back foot before catching a lift so you are less likely to hurt yourself if you fall.

🏔 Don't rock the lift and always remember to pull down the safety bar. Make sure your front foot is firmly strapped in before you get on and take care of others as you get off.

If you want to get the best out of your equipment you have to look after it. Your board and **bindings** should be serviced professionally once a year, but there are also a few things you can do yourself to keep it running smoothly. Caring for a board is not easy and it's best to ask an expert for help.

Waxing the board

The board will travel faster if it's waxed regularly.

1 Using an old iron (not a steam iron), melt some snowboard wax onto the board.

2 Spread it evenly with the iron.

3 Let the wax cool, then use a scraper to file off the excess, leaving just a thin layer.

WARNING: never try this without the help of an adult.
NEVER use a steam iron.

Sharpening the edges

If the edges of the board are not sharp it will effect your turning ability, so use a file to smooth out any rough bits. Keep the file square on to the edge and make sure you file along the whole length of the edge, or it can become uneven.

Bindings

Check your bindings every day when boarding. Wear and tear can loosen screws and damage straps and if these come undone as you're riding it can be dangerous. Always carry a **mini driver** and a spare set of binding bolts just in case.

Boots

During a hard day's boarding, your boots will get wet. Water can penetrate through the stitching of the boots, so it helps to use a waterproofing spray. Boot linings should be taken out and dried, but don't put them directly on top of a radiator or they will dry too quickly and it could damage the leather. If the boots are very wet put newspaper inside to soak up moisture.

Clothing

Don't throw your clothes in a damp heap when you finish boarding for the day. There is nothing worse than going back out onto the slope in damp, smelly gear – if you do you will not stay warm for long.

 TOP TIP

When you have finished riding for the season, don't just dump your board in the garage and forget about it. Boards rust and warp in damp conditions, so it's better to keep them in a warm place and cover them with a thick layer of wax.

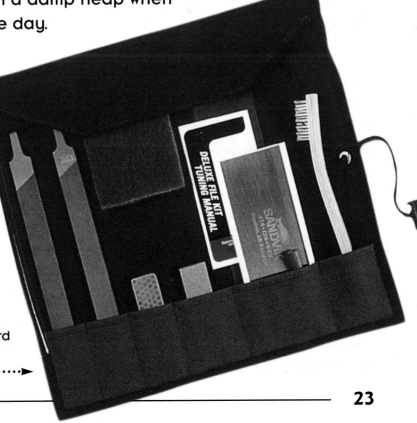

You'll need a selection of files to keep the edges of your board sharp and smooth.

SAFETY FIRST

The rules of the slopes

The basic rule of snowboarding is to have fun without putting yourself or others at risk.

- Stick to the marked **piste** at all times. The off-piste area is not patrolled or prepared and there may be dangerous trees, rocks, avalanches or even **crevasses** lying in wait for the unsuspecting boarder.

- Never attempt anything you are not ready for. As you improve you will become more adventurous but if you want to jump, build up to it slowly. Never jump off anything unless you know there is a safe landing on the other side.

Warning signs mean danger so don't ignore them. This sign tells riders the piste ahead is closed. Anyone going beyond the rope is putting themselves at risk.

- Keep your distance from other skiers and boarders. Sometimes they can change direction unexpectedly and if you are too close you will not have time to avoid them. Remember that the rider in front always has priority.

- Before you turn always have a quick look up the slope to make sure you will not cross the path of anyone coming down at speed. Never stop suddenly without checking whether anyone is behind you and always stop in an area where people coming from behind will be able to see you. If you want to rest make sure you stop on the edge of the piste.

- Slow down early as you approach a lift queue. If you try to stop at the last minute and make a mistake you could end up getting hurt or hurting others. Don't cut into lift queues – this is one of the most annoying things any skier or boarder can do.

- Don't go too fast in beginners' areas. Even if you think you're in control, others may not be.

- Keep your **lift pass** safe. If you lose it, you will have to pay for another one. Make sure you know when the lifts close. If you try to catch a last run around closing time you could find yourself stranded on the mountain.

Keep your wits about you when approaching a lift queue. Skiers and boarders will often be converging from different directions so slow down well in advance.

SNOWBOARDING EVENTS

There are a number of snowboarding contests that give the stars a chance to shine. Some are part of a world tour and others are just demonstration events, but there are often big prizes at stake. Competitions are not just confined to ski resorts – a few take place in specially-created arenas in the middle of cities that hardly ever see snow.

Halfpipe

The tricks of the **halfpipe** evolved from skateboarding and surfing. Riders take it in turns to go down the pipe, crossing from one wall to the other and doing jumps and spins off each side. A panel of judges chooses the winner.

Snowboardcross

In a **snowboardcross** event, groups of four to six riders race downhill against each other over a course of bumps, gates, jumps and banked turns. The competition is run in heats and the best riders go head-to-head in a grand final. Physical contact between riders is allowed, but they are not allowed to push or shove with their shoulders.

Canadian Russ Rebagliati on his way to winning gold in the giant **slalom** at the 1998 winter Olympics. His tight clothing and **alpine** board give him extra speed.

Slalom

In giant slalom riders take it in turns to race down a course of 25 gates, each placed about 20 metres apart. The winner is the rider who clocks the fastest time. There is also a dual slalom event, in which two riders race side by side down parallel courses and the best time over two runs wins.

 Music is a very important part of the snowboarding scene and you will always hear tunes blasting out of the speakers at competitions. Boarders' favourites include dance music, hip hop and drum and bass.

Other events

In **slope style** contests, competitors ride over a series of different jumps and are judged on the quality of their tricks and manoeuvres. There are also **quarterpipe** contests, where riders use just one curved wall for jumps rather than two. But perhaps the most daring of all are the **big air** contests. Riders take it in turns to launch themselves off a big jump and are judged for the style of their trick.

A fearless rider spins high above the ground in a big air contest. Top boarders spend hours practising in order to impress the judges with the most spectacular trick.

THE INTERNATIONAL SCENE

Everyone has their favourite boarder, but here is a selection of top riders currently setting their sport alight.

Marguerite Cossettini (Australia)

Marguerite became the first women's **snowboardcross** world champion in 1997 and won the title again the following year. She has been boarding since 1988 and was lucky to survive being caught in avalanches twice.

Sasha Ryzy (Australia)

A snowboardcross and **big air** expert, Sasha spends half the year racing in Australia and New Zealand and half competing in Canada, USA, Europe and Japan.

Nicola Thost (Germany)

Nicola started off as a skier but crossed over to boarding. It paid off when she became junior World Champion, then won the **halfpipe** gold medal at the 1998 winter Olympics.

Terje Haakonsen (Norway)

Freestyle master Terje has dominated the competition for years and consistently jumps more than 2.7 metres out of the halfpipe. He is so good that he once started a **slalom** course riding **fakie** (backwards) and still won.

Daniel Franck (Norway)

One of the very few riders to be able to boast that he beat Terje Haakonsen in a halfpipe competition.

Jamie Lynn (USA)

Jamie started off riding mountain bikes and skateboarding, but became one of the best boarders in the world. He is also a keen artist and surfer.

Melanie Leando shows the skills that made her the British halfpipe champion in 1998. She hopes to win a medal at the next winter Olympics. ••••••••••••••••••••••••➤

Jamie Phillp is one of the few British boarders with experience on the world circuit. He is a halfpipe specialist and has already starred in several snowboard action videos.

Michelle Taggart (USA)

A legend in the snowboarding world as world halfpipe champion for four years in a row.

Jamie Phillp (UK)

In the UK Jamie is the hottest prospect on the men's scene, having won the 1998 British overall championship at the age of just 17.

Lesley McKenna and Melanie Leando (UK)

Lesley and Melanie are Britain's top female boarders. They have set up the British Women's Snowboarding Team so they can take on the world's best.

Extreme events

There are some foolhardy riders out there who will go to any lengths to test their limits. The craziest of all extreme contests is the King of the Hill in Alaska. This four-day event involves a freestyle course of big jumps, a very tricky slalom and an extreme descent where the first rider to reach the bottom wins.

WARNING – this type of riding is extremely dangerous and even the best riders get hurt doing it.

Winter Olympics

Snowboarding showed how far it had come when it was chosen to become an Olympic medal event. So in 1998, at Nagano in Japan, riders competed for medals in slalom and halfpipe events.

GLOSSARY

alpine   a type of snowboarding done in hard boots that involves fast carving turns

big air   a contest in which riders do a big jump and try to pull off the best trick

bindings   devices used to attach the rider's feet to the board

button lift   a drag lift with a button-shaped plate which the boarder puts between his or her legs to catch a lift up the mountain

carve   to turn the board on its edge without sliding

crevasse   a gap in the mountainside

drag lift   a machine that pulls riders up the mountain on their boards

edging   digging the edge of the board into the snow to turn, slow down or stop

fakie   riding backwards

fall line   an imaginary line pointing straight down the hill

freeriding   snowboarding on all types of terrain for fun

freestyle   a type of snowboarding involving tricks and jumps

fun park   an area set aside for snowboarders to do freestyle tricks

goofy   a stance with the right foot in the forward position

halfpipe   a U-shaped trench on a downward slope used for freestyle snowboarding

hard boots   footwear used for alpine snowboarding

heeledge/heelside   the side of the board where the heels rest

leash   a safety device used to attach the board to the front foot so that it does not run away

lift pass   a pass that skiers and boarders pay for to use the lifts

mini driver   small screwdriver used to make adjustments to bindings

nose   the front tip of the snowboard

plate-binding   a flat plate used to connect hard boots to an alpine board

P-tex   clear material that makes up the flat running surface of the snowboard

piste   a run of compacted snow on a mountain

quarterpipe   similar to a halfpipe but riders use just one curved wall for jumps rather than two

regular   stance with left foot in the forward position

scooting   propelling the board along on flat terrain with the back foot free and the front foot in the binding

side-slip   moving downhill with the board facing directly across the slope and the boarder using the uphill edge to control speed

ski lift   used to transport boarders and skiers up the mountain

slalom   a snowboarding event involving zigzagging down a course of gates

slope style   a contest in which riders go off a range of different jumps and are judged on their tricks

snowboardcross   a downhill race with boarders competing side-by-side over a course of bumps and gates

Snurfer   a toy for riding on snow which inspired the development of boarding

soft boots   footwear for freestyle or freeride snowboarding

stance   the position of the feet on the snowboard

step-in binding   a catch system for attaching boot to board by just stepping onto the board

stomp mat   non-slip pad attached to the board between the bindings to stop the rear foot from slipping when getting on and off lifts

tail   the rear tip of the snowboard

toe-edge/toeside   the edge of the snowboard where the toes rest

T-bar   T-shaped drag lift that pulls the rider up the slope

traversing   riding the board across the slope on the toeside or heelside edge

twin-tip   a board with an identically-shaped nose and tail

uphill edge   the edge of the board that is highest up the slope as the rider is traversing

wrist guards   supportive gear to stop the wrists getting hurt in a fall

A snowboarder's terms

The vocabulary of snowboarding is weird and wonderful. Here are a few bizarre words and phrases that you might expect to hear on the slopes.

to bail – to fall over
to boost – to catch air off a jump

burger flip, Canadian bacon air, chicken salad air, flying squirrel air, roast beef air, Swiss cheese air – types of snowboard tricks
fat air – big air
grommet – a dedicated, young snowboarder
sick – very good
stoked – very excited

USEFUL ADDRESSES

Associations

British Snowboard Association (BSA)
First Floor
4 Trinity Square
Llandudno
North Wales
LL30 2PY
01492 872540

International Snowboard Federation (ISF)
Pradlerstrasse 21
A6020 Innsbruck
Austria
00 43 512 343 834 16

United States Snowboard Association (USASA)
315 East Alcott Avenue
Fergus Falls
Minnesota
MN 56537
00 1 218 739 4716

Snowboard Australia
Suite 323
656 Military Road
Mosman
NSW 2088
sba@zip.com.au

Places to snowboard

Despite the general lack of snow in Britain, there are plenty of artificial ski slopes where you can learn to snowboard. You can find artificially-made snow to ride on at the Tamworth Snow Dome, which has a 150-metre indoor slope (tel 0990 000011)

Many European resorts are excellent for boarders and have **fun parks** reserved for boarders to practise their tricks. Among the best are:
Avoriaz and Les Arcs (France)
Ischgl and Axamer Lizum (Austria)
Leysin and Laax (Switzerland)
Courmayeur (Italy)

Top North American resorts include:
Telluride, Mammoth and Breckenridge (USA)
Lake Louise and Whistler (Canada)

Board repair (UK centres)

Snowboard Klinik advice and repair centre
01543 473444

FURTHER READING

Books

World Snowboard Guide,
Ice Publishing
(up-to-date reviews of snowboard resorts across the globe)

Snowboard Bible,
Air Publications Ltd
(all-round guide to snowboarding)

Magazines

Snowboard UK, Air Publications

White Lines, Permanent Publishing

Fall Line, Fall Line Ltd

Websites

www.Isf.ch (ISF website with access to BSA website)

www.globalsnowboard.com (Snowboard UK website)

www.board-x.com (website of Britain's premier snowboard festival)

www.klinik.co.uk (Snowboard Klinik website)

www.solsnowboarding.com (USA snowboard website)

www.twsnow.com (USA snowboard website)

www.snowboardaustralia.org.au

INDEX